©2011 Rachel Inbar   Is Commercial Cord Blood Banking Ethical?

Is Commercial Cord Blood Banking Ethical?

Table of Contents

1 Introduction 4

2 Cord blood 7

    2.1 What is cord blood? 7

    2.2 Storage and use of cord blood 8

    2.3 Making the decision whether to bank cord blood for autologous use / in a private cord blood bank 9

    2.4 Cost of private cord blood banking 10

    2.5 Criticism of commercial cord blood banking......................10

3 Ethical aspects of private cord blood banking..........................11

    3.1 Medical Ethics 11

        3.1.1 Patient autonomy / Informed consent 11

        3.1.2 Beneficence and non-maleficence 12

        3.1.3 Justice..12

    3.2 Immanuel Kant – The Categorical Imperative 12

    3.3 John Rawls – Justice 13

    3.4 Ethical questions arising from commercial cord blood banking 14

    3.5 Effects of manipulative advertising on informed consent 15

	3.5.1	Manipulative advertising 15
	3.5.2	Informed consent..18
	3.5.3	Patient autonomy 20

    3.6   Manipulative advertising and the exploitation of vulnerability 20

	3.6.1	Exploiting vulnerability...20
	3.6.2	Beneficence and non-maleficence 22
	3.6.3	Justice..23

4   Discussion 26

5   Summary..31

6   Bibliography...33

1 Introduction

The first successful cord blood transplant was performed (Burgio, Gluckman, & Locatelli, 2003), showing the use of cord blood to be a viable alternative to bone marrow transplant (Rubinstein, 2006). Gradually, over the past several decades, and with the increase in medical evidence as to the usefulness of cord blood, its status has gone from medical waste, discarded without a second thought, to a lifesaving treasure (Rei, 2010).

The collection of cord blood must be done by a trained professional, but is fairly simple and is considered by most to be risk-free (Gonzalez-Ryan, Van Syckle, Coyne, & Glove, 2000). If tested (for hepatitis B, HIV, etc.) and typed (for HLA) prior to freezing, the cord blood unit has logistical advantages, as it can be thawed when needed and is available almost immediately (Rubinstein, 2006; Saginur, Kharaboyan, & Knoppers, 2004).

Private cord blood banks give promises of "biological insurance" and encourage parents to store their newborn's cord blood – a procedure that is a "once in a lifetime opportunity" that must be performed almost immediately after birth (Sullivan, 2008; Ballen, Barker, Stewart, Greene, & Lane, 2008). These banks store the blood for autologous (self) or family use, for cases in which the child herself or a family member contracts a disease it is able to help cure.

Autologous use, however, is extremely rare. In fact, a child with leukemia or genetic diseases cannot receive an autologous transfer, as the precursors of the disease exist in the stem cells and therefore cannot be used to cure the patient (Brand, et al., 2008). Statistics show the likelihood of an autologous transfer being the best solution for a sick child in the first 20 years of life to be around somewhere in the range of 1 in 2500 to 1 in 200,000 (Ballen, et al., 2008).

Providing a service that is highly unlikely to ever be beneficial raises interesting ethical questions that I hope to answer in this paper, with the main question being whether private cord banking can be justified according to the standards of medical ethics, according to Kant's Categorical Imperative and according to Rawls' Theory of Justice.

I start this paper with a brief explanation of what cord blood is and its advantages over other alternatives available to patients. I then discuss the problematic issues faced by parents during their decision-making process, how these problems are further intensified by commercial cord blood banks and the ways in which the actions of such banks meet or fail to meet ethical standards.

One of the main ethical questions I raise is that of justice, and whether or not it is promoted by commercial cord blood banks. As the initial costs of opening and operating a cord blood bank are significant, I discuss whether it can be ethically justified to combine private (commercial) banking with public banking in order to offset the costs, thus providing a potentially life-saving service that might not otherwise be available.

I conclude this paper with the ways in which I believe commercial cord blood banks **can** be operated so that they comply with the standards of medical ethics, Kant's Categorical Imperative and

Rawls' Theory of Justice, until such time as governments step in to provide support (or greater support) for public cord blood banking.

2 Cord blood

2.1 What is cord blood?

Cord blood is blood collected from the umbilical cord and placenta within a very short time after a baby's birth (Ballen, et al., 2008). In general, the procedure of cord blood banking is non-invasive and is considered to be absent of risk (Saginur, et al., 2004). It can, however, bear a low risk for the newborn if the umbilical cord is clamped too soon after birth. In such a case, the newborn is at risk for reduced blood volume and possible anemia (Banking Your Newborn's Cord Blood, 2010). Premature babies who have a particularly low volume of blood in their placenta and umbilical cord are poor candidates for cord blood banking, as the sample collected would have insufficient stem cells to be useful.

Cord blood contains hematopoietic (blood-forming) cells similar to those found in bone marrow, making it a transplant alternative in cases in which radiation and chemotherapy are used to kill diseased cells. The hematopoietic cells operate as a repair system for the body by producing healthy blood cells to replace those killed during treatment (Banking Your Newborn's Cord Blood, 2010; Saginur et. al., 2004).

Cord blood transplants have two main advantages over bone marrow transplants: a lower risk of graft vs. host disease (GvHD) (Rubinstein, 2006), and the immediate availability of the sample once a match is determined (Saginur et. al., 2004).

2.2 Storage and use of cord blood

After processing, stem cells from the cord blood are stored frozen (cryopreserved) (Ballen, et al., 2008), to be thawed when needed. Two types of banks exist – public banks, in which the blood is typed and used whenever it is found to match a person in need (allogeneic use) and private or family banks, in which the blood is stored for personal (autologous) use or the use of close family members (Fisk, Roberts, Markwald, & Mironov, 2005).

Allogeneic transplants (both from related and unrelated donors) are recognized as an effective form of therapy for multiple medical conditions (Gonzalez-Ryan, et al., 2000; Rubinstein, 2006; Fernandez et al., 2003), but the value of banking cord blood for autologous use is highly debated (Ballen, et al., 2008). The probability of autologous use in a family with no history of blood disease is extremely low – approximately 1 in 20,000 (Burgio, et al., 2003). One of the reasons for the infrequent use of autologous cord blood transfers is the fact that banked cord blood carries the same mutation found in inherited disorders and therefore cannot be used to cure its donor (Saginur, et. al., 2004) or, simply stated, "Autologous transplantation is not suited for the treatment of genetic disorders." (Schmidt, Platz, Rutt, & Ehninger, 2010, p. 234)

Rubinstein (2006) notes that the "private, 'just in case' or speculative storage of cord blood for potential use in either autologous or related transplants so far has helped solve very few clinical situations." (p. 399). Schmidt et.al., (2010) responding to Hollands and McCauley (2009) state that "in the vast majority of cases where an HLA-identical cord blood unit that was stored in a private bank is available for transplantation, an HLA-identical related bone marrow transplantation from the same donor would also be possible." (p. 234) In the same article, Schmidt et.al., (2010) also challenge the assertion that future scientific developments will cause cord blood to be more useful in the future by providing examples of current scientific developments that are likely to make the use of cord blood entirely obsolete.

2.3   Making the decision whether to bank cord blood for autologous use / in a private cord blood bank

As cord blood can only be drawn in the minutes following birth of a baby, parents must decide prior to the child's birth if they are interested in banking the child's cord blood. A special withdrawal kit is used and a maximal amount of available blood is collected (Banking Your Newborn's Cord Blood, 2010). Cord blood that is not collected shortly after birth is no longer usable.

Parent's motivation to bank cord blood

Parents often decide to bank their newborn's cord blood because they have another child or a close relative with a disease than can be treated using a bone marrow transplant. Interestingly, a cord blood transplant can only be performed on children or young adults, as the amount of stem cells is insufficient to complete a transplant for an adult. (Banking Your Newborn's Cord Blood, 2010)

In families where there is no history of blood disease that could possibly be aided by using cord blood, parents often make the decision to bank their newborns' cord blood based on claims made by the cord blood banks, regarding the prospects of future use. In a study of 442 women regarding attitudes toward cord blood banking, of the women who would have preferred private banking (over public banking), 90% stated that it would be a "good investment in case (the) child needs it" (p. 697) and 62% answered that they anticipated feelings of guilt if the child needed cord blood and they had chosen not to store it (Fernandez, Gordon, Van den Hof, Taweel, & Baylis, 2003).

2.4   Cost of private cord blood banking

The cost of private cord blood banking is approximately $1000 - $2000 in addition to a yearly fee of approximately $100. The withdrawal kit, courier service to the blood bank and the separation of stem cells and preparation for cryopreservation may cost several hundred dollars more (Banking Your Newborn's Cord Blood, 2010).

2.5   Criticism of commercial cord blood banking

"Medical professional societies have repeatedly expressed their reservations about parents who, despite exhibiting no risk of related conditions store their children's cord blood for the family's or the children's own needs." (Rei, 2010, p. 6) The French National Consultative Ethics Committee is quoted as saying that private banks, "contradict the principle of solidarity, without which no society can survive." (Rei, 2010, p. 7) Rei (2010) goes on to say that the underlying market forces that affect cord blood banking in Taiwan "erode the possibility of a more altruistic society" (p. 17).

France has put severe limitations on commercial (for-profit) cord blood banking and Italy has completely banned it (Cord Blood Bank; Brand, et al., 2008). Many organizations including the American Academy of Pediatrics and the World Marrow Donor Association have openly criticized the practice of commercial cord blood banking (Sullivan, 2008).

3 Ethical aspects of private cord blood banking

In this paper, I have chosen to examine the ethical aspects of private cord blood banking according to the guidelines of medical ethics, Kant's Categorical Imperative and Rawls' Theory of Justice. I will explain each of these briefly and then discuss them in depth in the context of cord blood banking.

3.1 Medical Ethics

Firms running cord blood banks are subject not only to general ethical requirements, but they also must answer to medical ethic requirements. These can either legitimize or delegitimize the actions of firms operating in the medical arena, acting as criteria for whether decisions can be regarded as ethical or not.

Values that apply to medical ethics and are relevant to this discussion include patient autonomy and informed consent, beneficence and non-maleficence and justice (Beauchamp, 2003). I will describe each of these briefly.

3.1.1 Patient autonomy / Informed consent

According to accepted medical ethic practices, patient autonomy provides patients who are capable of doing so with the right to choose or refuse treatments (Values in medical ethics). Autonomy, however requires that patients (or, in this case, parents acting on behalf of their child) make decisions based on objective information (Schmidt, et al., 2010), a concept referred to as informed consent.

Informed consent requires that prior to agreeing to (or deciding against) treatment, a patient (or someone acting on his or her behalf) is fully informed about the risks and potential benefits of the treatment (Values in medical ethics). True patient autonomy can only exist when medical procedures are fully and truthfully explained.

3.1.2 Beneficence and non-maleficence

Beneficence, according to Beauchamp (2003) refers to the obligation to provide benefit that outweighs the associated risks and non-maleficence is the corresponding obligation to avoid causing the patient harm.

3.1.3 Justice

Justice refers to the obligation to fairly distribute medical resources, including decisions regarding treatment priorities – i.e., who will be treated first if resources do not allow for treatment of all patients in a similar position (Values in medical ethics; Beauchamp, 2003).

3.2 Immanuel Kant – The Categorical Imperative

Among the most well-known moral philosophers is Immanuel Kant who lived in the 18th century. Kant's theory of moral behavior states that there is a single moral obligation, the "Categorical Imperative". According to Kant, categorical imperative means that moral obligations are both absolute and unconditional; they cannot based on the wills or desires of individuals (Wikipedia, Immanuel Kant). Kant's approach is deontological (Geva, 2000), attributing the value of an action to the motivation for performing it (as opposed to the teleological approach, which attributes the value of an action to its outcome). On the basis of this theory, Kant stated the following maxims:

1. **The universal maxim**: "Act only on that maxim through which you can at the same time will it should become a universal law." (Immanuel Kant) – "The maxim upon which one's actions are based — no matter how complex — must be such that anyone in exactly the same circumstances should be able to act upon it. It should be universal in the sense of applying to all human beings in that particular set of circumstances." (Veatch, 1972)
2. **Humans as ends maxim**: Treat all people as an end in themselves, and never only as a means to an end. (Geva, 2000)

3.3   John Rawls – Justice

Aristotle proposed a formal definition of justice, according to which the share an individual receives should be based on his merits. He went on to define two types of justice – distributive and retributive. Questions of distributive justice arise when a common (in the sense of belonging to a group) resource cannot be distributed among all those who could benefit from it. In such cases, guidelines must be created as a basis for just distribution. (Geva, 2000)

John Rawls is an American philosopher whose book "A Theory of Justice" is considered a milestone book (A Theory of Justice; John Rawls) outlined principles of justice, prioritizing them according to the order in which they should be applied when they conflict with one another (Justice as Fairness).

The principles are:

1. **The Liberty Principle**, which states that each individual has a right to basic liberties.
2. **The Equality Principle**, which states that social and economic inequalities should be arranged to provide the greatest benefit to the least advantaged.
3. **The Original Position**, which claims that the Principles of Justice mentioned above would be those selected by people in the "original position" (Justice as Fairness) – "a state in which no person is aware of his place in society, his wealth, talents, personal characteristics or even his own perception of good" (Geva, 2000, p. 148). In such a case a person is expected to make a decision that would be good for him regardless of what position in society he actually ends up having.

3.4 Ethical questions arising from commercial cord blood banking

Public cord banking has well-accepted advantages (Schmidt, et al., 2010) that are beyond the scope of this paper. In this paper I will discuss the ethical aspects of private, commercial cord blood banking. The main question this paper aims to answer is – Is it ethical for cord blood banks to offer parents the opportunity to privately store their newborn's cord blood, knowing that the odds of actually using the sample for his/her own use in the future are extremely small?

I have identified the following four ethical questions that I feel need to be answered in order to answer the main question: 1) Do commercial cord blood banks present scientifically-based information that enables soon-to-be parents to make an educated decision that qualifies as informed consent with regard to banking their newborn's cord blood? In cases in which informed consent is achieved, does commercial blood banking support parents' rights to autonomy? 2) Do commercial cord blood banks exploit the vulnerability of soon-to-be parents by giving them messages encouraging an emotional (rather than logical) decision? 3) Does banking cord blood for autologous use meet the conditions of beneficence and non-maleficence? 4) Is it legitimate for cord blood banks to provide the opportunity for parents who have the financial means to store their newborn's cord blood – is this a just division of medical resources?

"The legitimacy of private banks should not be taken as a given." (Saginur, et al., 2004, p. 22)

Although there do exist a minority of cases in which cryo-preservation of blood is a medically sound decision (explained in the Beneficence and Non-Maleficence section below), in the vast majority of other cases, the decision to privately store cryopreserved cord blood does not make obvious sense, based on statistics of future use. If so, why do parents make the decision to bank their newborn's cord blood?

3.5 Effects of manipulative advertising on informed consent

3.5.1 Manipulative advertising

Cord blood banks entice soon-to-be parents with various promises such as "biologic insurance" (Annas, 1999), "Experience a lifetime of security" (Family Cord), "We know that expectant parents choose family cord blood banking because they want to do everything they can to protect their family." (Why Choose CORD:USE Cord Blood Bank) and "A promise. The moment you learn you are going to be a parent you make a promise to nurture, teach and most of all, to protect a life – your child's. Banking your newborn's cord blood …helps you keep that promise." (Why bank cord blood?).

"The promise of future use, by a family without a history of a disease that hematopoietic cells could be used to treat, seems unrealistic…" (Annas, 1999, p. 1524). Ballen, et al., (2008) estimate the autologous use of cord blood as occurring even more rarely - in as few as 1:200,000 collections. In many of these cases, it would actually be more effective to treat the person with the cells of an unrelated donor (Annas, 1999). The increasing medical expertise in unrelated transplantation, according to Gonzalez-Ryan et al., (2000), along with poor outcomes achieved by autologous transplantations, lead many experts to believe that storing cord blood for autologous use may be futile. The American Academy of Pediatrics also does not recommend autologous banking due to, "its investigational status as a stem cell source, limited indication of autologous banking, and low likelihood of future expansion." (AAP, 1999 in Gonzalez-Ryan et. al., 2000, p. 106). Codgell (2009) feels that the marketing schemes used by private cord blood banks are "a misleading effort to encourage parents to spend large sums of money to bank their child's cord blood for often futile purposes." (p. 150).

Autologous transplants are not in routine clinical use for many of the conditions that appear in private cord blood bank marketing materials (Sullivan, 2008). Sullivan (2008) further mentions that in 15 years of commercial cord blood banking, medical literature reports only a *single case* of autologous cord blood transplantation for acute lymphocytic leukemia (ALL) – a case that was later criticized as possibly having been the wrong treatment choice, made due to the availability of the cryopreserved cord blood as opposed to its being the best solution for the patient. To illustrate the likelihood of ever using an autologous cord blood sample, Sullivan (2008) presents the few cases in which such a sample could actually be used (e.g., acquired aplastic anemia), then takes the proportion of people who would be not cured by conventional methods, from those he removes those who cannot be cured using allogeneic cord blood transplants or bone marrow. His conclusion is that the odds of an autologous transfer being **the** cure for the condition are extremely small (less than 1:200,000).

The advertising messages, therefore, are not only misleading, they may fall under the category of coercion described by Beauchamp (1992). Do these messages threaten with negative sanctions, as required by Beauchamp in order to qualify as coercive? I believe that they do, at least to some extent, as they imply that *not* banking cord blood is disregarding a parent's responsibility to do everything possible to protect his child's life. If not protecting your child's life can be perceived as endangering your child's life, it is undoubtedly a negative outcome. Even if these messages may not be perceived by some as coercive, they discuss incentives and use emotional pressure and are undoubtedly manipulative (Beauchamp, 1992).

"Manipulation is an attempt to induce one to believe what is not correct, unsound, or not backed by good reasons." (Beauchamp,

1992, p. 478) Saginur et al., (2004) discuss their concern over the accuracy and balance of information presented in donor solicitation and advertising methods geared toward prospective parents. The inaccurate information often promises future use, such as regenerative medicine – a technology that has not yet been demonstrated even in medical trials (Samuel, Kerridge, & O'Brien, 2008).

A respected news magazine, Maclean's, ran an article that referred to umbilical cord blood as useful for battling leukemia and genetic disorders (Saginur et al., 2004). This example of misinformation in a respected news magazine leads to the question, "… how can we expect soon-to-be parents, who are in a vulnerable phase wanting to do everything for their child, to be able to piece together a balanced and accurate picture?" (Saginur et al., 2004, p. 31).

3.5.2 Informed consent

Informed consent requires that a person making a decision be competent and well-informed and s/he must not be coerced or pressured (Bourque & Sugarman, 2000). Understanding the crucial differences between private and public cord blood banking requires, according to Sullivan (2008) knowledge beyond that of the majority of lay people. Clearly, in order to make an informed decision, the parents must be presented with actual odds that an autologous transplant would hold unique advantages for the child for whom it is being saved.

According to Gonzalez-Ryan et al. (2000), informed consent is the most crucial concern of private cord blood banking. They describe the information needed by consumers in order to make informed decisions as including the risks of the collection procedure, privacy issues arising from extensive testing performed on the sample and potential uses and limitations of the collected sample – including the likelihood of use. For example, parents should be aware of the fact that should their child develop a malignancy, the child would be more likely to benefit from the transplant from a healthy donor, rather than from his own cryopreserved stem cells. In addition, the limited number of stem cells in stored samples makes such samples useable only for patients weighing less than 50kg.

In answer to my first question, I believe that commercial cord blood banks often fail to present scientifically-based information that could enable soon-to-be parents to make an educated decision with regard to banking their newborn's cord blood that would qualify as informed consent.

One additional point I feel it is important to mention is that people's decisions are not always rational. Multiple studies on decision under risk have documented people's tendency to overestimate low probabilities (Wu & Gonzalez, 1999). "(as) people are limited in their ability to comprehend and evaluate extreme probabilities, highly unlikely events are either ignored or overweighted…" (Kahneman & Tversky, 1979, pp. 282-283). This may make the likelihood of actually being able to use the cord blood for autologous use (even after being provided with accurate data) seem greater to the parents than it actually is. In a study performed by Fernandez, et. al (2003), a fourth of the respondents overestimated the probability of a child needing a bone marrow transplant before age 10.

3.5.3 Patient autonomy

If parents have received truthful, accurate information and have the financial means to pay for the collection and storage of cord blood, then cord blood banks indeed support the value of providing patients or those acting on their behalf with the autonomy to make an informed medical decision. If no option of public cord blood banking exists, this can be seen as an advantage of private cord blood banking. In cases of directed banking (explained later), the absence of such an option could be considered detrimental.

3.6 Manipulative advertising and the exploitation of vulnerability

3.6.1 Exploiting vulnerability

As the collection of cord blood must occur only very shortly after birth of a newborn, parents must make the decision prior to birth (assuming that a collection kit and a person with the knowledge required to collect the sample must be present in the delivery room) (Cells For Life, 2011). This is a time-period during which parents are particularly vulnerable (Annas, 1999). A promise of biologic insurance – the once-in-a-lifetime opportunity to possibly save their child at some point in the future (Fisk, Roberts, Markwald, & Mironov, 2005; Ballen, Barker, Stewart, Greene, & Lane, 2008) -- combined with the pressure to make a time-limited decision -- can be seen as deeply exploitative of the vulnerability of parents (Annas, 1999).

Fisk et al., (2005) ask sarcastically, questioning the exploitative aspects of cord blood bank practices, "Even at a typical cost of several thousand dollars, how could any responsible parent fail to provide for their child's future by preserving "something that may conceivably save his or her life?"" (pp. 87-88).

Frequent media campaigns ask potential bone marrow donors to provide blood samples, to enable their HLA phenotypes to be added to a national or international registry. Accompanied with testimony provided by patients and their families regarding the fact that no suitable donor has been located, these pleas may have an emotional effect on parents who hope to avoid a similar situation. These campaigns are not misleading - 70% of people in need of a bone marrow transplant are unable to locate a suitable donor (The Nuts and Bolts of Bone Marrow Transplants). Sullivan (2008) views the marketing efforts of commercial cord banks as "guilt-tripping" the parents into doing what is best for their child by stating that storing their cord blood could save their life at some point in the future. Professional groups too have argued that cord blood banks use powerful advertising to sell possible future uses of umbilical cord blood, capitalizing on parental anxiety (Sugarman, et al., 1997 in Samuel, et al., 2008). As pediatric nurses, Gonzalez-Ryan et al., (2000) conclude, "We must advocate for parents, may who find it difficult to resist public pressure to optimize an opportunity that may not be for everyone." (p. 110).

Gonzalez-Ryan et al., (2000) also raise the question as to whether it is ethical to ask parents to "make a large financial investment for a potentially unfeasible procedure". (p. 110) Lack of feasibility includes those points mentioned above, in addition to the viability of the collected cells at the time when they need to be used – it is unknown how many of the cells will in fact survive, particularly when a long period of time (over 15 years) has passed (Broxmeyer, Srour, Hangoc, Cooper, Anderson, & Bodine, 2003).

In answer to my second question, I believe that commercial cord blood banks do exploit the vulnerability of soon-to-be parents by giving them messages encouraging an emotional (rather than logical, information-based) decision.

3.6.2   Beneficence and non-maleficence

In terms of non-maleficence, cord blood banking involves a donation that is absent of pain or risk to the donor (Saginur, et al., 2004) and therefore is in accordance with this criterion. In a review by Veatch (1991) of Marsh and Yarborough's (1990) book "Medicine and Money: A Study of the Role of Beneficence in Health Care Cost Containment", Veatch cites Marsh and Yarborough as saying that expenditures for futile care do patients more harm than good (Veatch R. , 1991). In this case, once we agree that autologous transfers, when there is no history or knowledge of blood diseases, have only negligible odds of ever being used, we can also agree that storage of such samples is futile and therefore does not qualify as beneficent.

In families in which there are known medical issues that can be treated with the help of a future hematopoietic stem cell transplant (e.g., an HLA-matching sibling who has leukemia), banking the cord blood is often ordered by clinicians (Warwick & Fehily, 2002; Brand, et al., 2008). This type of collection, known as "directed" (Warwick & Fehily, 2002), is recommended by The American Academy of Pediatrics (Cogdell, 2009). In fact, it would be unwise for a family with prior knowledge of such an illness to dispose of the valuable cord blood (Sullivan, 2008). If cord blood cryo-preservation is not available in a public bank, it is obviously to the family's advantage to have the opportunity to bank their newborn's cord blood privately – and therefore beneficent. It should be noted, however, that a fully-matched sibling could also donate bone marrow in lieu of the cord blood (Sullivan, 2008), although clearly it is a more complicated procedure, involving greater risk. It is also interesting to note that some private companies store directed cord blood samples free of charge (Grady, 1998).

To summarize, in answer to my third question, banking cord blood is non-maleficent and banking *for directed use* also meets the conditions of beneficence, although banking for autologous use does not.

3.6.3 Justice

Saginur, et al. (2004) raise the concern that autologous cord blood banking leads to societal inequities, suggesting that only public cord blood banks should be encouraged and that if, at some point in the future, autologous use of cord blood becomes a viable and reasonable treatment alternative, then the public sector should take the financial responsibility required for its storage. This is no different from access to other types of healthcare (Bourque & Sugarman, 2000). As of 2008, the National Marrow Donor Program in the USA reported that cord blood units from public banks were used 650 times more frequently than were units from private banks. Ironically, substantially more units are stored in private than in public banks. (Rei, 2010)

Many authors (e.g., Annas, 1999; Gonzalez-Ryan et al., 2000) have addressed the issue of the legal status of cord blood. Annas (1999) discusses the fact that, in the past, cord and placental blood were considered waste. He raises two possible analogies that can be assigned to cord blood – organ transplantation and blood donation. Organ transplantation holds risks for the donor and a "gift relationship" generally exists between the donor and the recipient. Blood transfusions, on the other hand, hold minimal risks for the donor and therefore sale of blood has been allowed (as opposed to organs, the sale of which is forbidden in most countries). Cord blood is more similar to blood than to an organ in terms of risks for the donor, and therefore should have the same legal standing as blood. In either case, according to Gluckman (1996), there is an implicit agreement within the health care community that blood and organs, which are freely donated, should not be used for profit (in Ferreira, Pasternak, Bacal, de Campos Guerra & Watanabe, 1999). Annas (1999) believes that the newborn's mother undoubtedly has the authority to make the decision regarding what should be done with the cord blood – as long as her choices are reasonable in terms of medical practice. He goes on to say that once value can be attributed to cord blood (i.e., it is considered property), the mother must be informed of this fact and she must consent to whatever use is to be made of the cord blood (whether research, public banking or other).

Knowing that allogeneic transfers are both more common and more successful, it follows that individuals privately banking cord blood are, in fact, holding a resource that is far more likely to be useful for the general public than for themselves, raising an ethical question.

"A distribution mechanism will be deemed untenable if its prescriptions are significantly at variance with observed ethical judgments." (Yaari & Bar-Hillel, 1984). The ethical judgments involved in private possession of a medical resource that could possibly save the life of an unrelated patient should it become available to him or her – particularly when it is of no use to its owner – are undoubtedly complicated and, unfortunately, beyond the scope of this paper. I will, however, note that Rei (2010) and Fisk et al. (2005) are concerned that "misplaced enthusiasm for commercial auto-collection will undermine the proven utility of altruistic public cord blood banks." (p. 88).

I feel that in order to answer my fourth question, regarding the just division of medical resources, a further analysis must be performed. I will do so in the discussion section of this paper, with the help of Immanuel Kant and John Rawls' theories.

4 Discussion

Let us begin by taking a look at the picture from the point of view of Kant's Categorical Imperative. According to the universal maxim, the person or organization responsible for opening a cord blood bank would need to accept someone else (or another organization) acting in the same way. Perhaps we can ask the question, "Would the owner of a cord blood bank bank his newborn's blood for autologous use (in a bank not owned by him)?" This would have to be based on two additional assumptions: first, there are no known medical conditions in the family for which its storage would be recommended and second, his financial situation is similar to the average financial situation of people in the area in which his cord blood operates. I believe it is important to include the financial situation as it seems more likely that people for whom storage of cord blood is a negligible expense might do so regardless of its expected utility. This can be exchanged with the question, "Does the person or organization deciding to open a private cord blood bank believe that cryo-preservation of cord blood for autologous use is a worthwhile investment?" If the answer to this question is yes, has adequate research been done? Is it not the responsibility of a person to sell a product or a service that has value? Goodpaster (1991) discusses the need for an organization to have a conscience and to treat its customers with respect. Treating customers with respect would require providing them with information sufficient to achieve informed consent. To this end, the bank itself would have to be aware of up-to-date medical research. With this knowledge, a decision to bank cord blood for autologous use would be an emotional decision rather than a rational one and the bank itself would be exploiting parents' emotional vulnerability.

If we agree that storing cord blood for autologous use, as The American Academy of Pediatrics states (AAP, 1999 in Gonzalez-Ryan et. al., 2000), is not recommended, due to it investigative status and low likelihood of being more useful in the future, then we can also agree that according to the universal maxim, we would not want all organizations to ask in the same way – encouraging us to "take out insurance" on situations that are extremely unlikely – and for which there are frequently other reasonable solutions. Even more so, it should be difficult for us to accept the emotional manipulation and the exploitation of vulnerability used to encourage us to do so.

It is difficult to consider the aspects of private cord blood banking without considering the alternatives (i.e., public banking or the use of bone marrow transplants from related or matched donors) and I believe this is an important part of the discussion. Rubinstein (2006), raises an interesting point when discussing the issue of funding for cord blood banks. A variety of costs are incurred when opening and operating a cord blood bank. Money is required for HLA typing, testing the samples for various illnesses, quality assurance, equipment, paying employees and multiple other costs. As it is widely accepted that cord blood has value for allogeneic use; the existence of public, non-commercial cord blood banks is not controversial (Fernandez, et al., 2003; Rei, 2010). Combining commercial (for-profit) cord blood banking with public cord blood banking, which is becoming increasingly popular (Rei, 2010), can serve to offset some of the costs, thus enabling the storage of cord blood samples for allogeneic use – which has the potential to help the general public, including the family storing cord blood for autologous use. This model enables the banks to operate until the needed samples are purchased (perhaps paid for by medical insurance) – at which time, the banks expect to establish a revenue stream (Rubinstein, 2006), thus solving the cash flow problem. In this model, a minority bears a majority of the cost, but the money works toward the common good.

Inspired by this quote - "While the chance of a donor benefiting may presently be low, this does not automatically mean that another member of society could not benefit." (Fisk, et al., 2005), and based on the evidence in favor of allogeneic transfers, I would like to consider the following hypothetical situation: Let us imagine that all cord blood samples are tested and typed in in the same way as is publicly banked cord blood. Now let us imagine a situation in which the parents are approached when the sample could be used to cure an unrelated person. If these parents agree, the sample is used and the insurance covers the costs paid by the parents. The parents could be refunded the costs they paid, perhaps less the storage costs incurred by the bank. This type of arrangement, which exists in Turkey, where private cord blood banks are required to offer 25% of the units they store for allogeneic use (Brand, et al., 2008) is beneficent. It, however, is not problem-free. It is not clear if people who banked their child's cord blood for autologous use would be willing to give it up. Surprisingly, in the Taiwan Genomic Survey performed in 2005, 63% of people were willing to store their newborn's cord blood. Of those, 92% stated that they would still be willing to donate the cord blood to save others (Rei, 2010). An additional problem is that the motivation to privately store cord blood is reduced as soon as parents feel they could acquire such a sample fairly easily, were they to ever need it – perhaps eliminating the same funding that could have been provided by private cord blood bankers.

According to Rawls' equality principle, private cord blood banking is unacceptable as it does not provide the greatest benefit to the least advantaged. Rather, traditional private cord blood banking (in which the samples are stored purely for autologous or family use), with the exception of directed banking, provides little or no benefit for *any* of the people banking cord blood.

To make private cord blood banking acceptable according to Rawls', private and public cord blood banking would be combined in the same bank, with the public samples being stored being those that are the most difficult types to come by. It is well-known that certain ethnic groups and racial minorities have the greatest difficulty finding matching samples (Banking Your Newborn's Cord Blood, 2010). Cord blood's primitive form requires a less exact match in order for transplantation to succeed (as compared to other types of hematopoietic stem cells), therefore storing samples from minority groups would provide them with a significantly greater chance of finding matches (Rei, 2010). The ethnic groups for whom matches are difficult to find are often underprivileged and have a lower socio-economic status. As such, even if the theoretical situation I illustrated above existed, and private banks worked similarly to public banks, offering allogeneic transfers to people determined as matches, people from these ethnic groups would be unlikely to be able to afford private cord blood banking, maintaining the same situation as that that currently exists – a lack of matching samples.

Ideally, governments would finance the initial costs associated with running a public cord blood bank, such as: the cost of equipment, supplies, HLA typing and personnel salaries (Rubinstein, 2006). However, until governments do make cord blood banking a priority, private cord blood banks – assuming they finance public banking as well, and make a concerted effort to specifically store samples from ethnic groups who are most desperate for them - have the potential to promote justice.

Promoting justice might be sufficient, even according to Kant's humans as ends maxim, which states that all people should be treated as an end in themselves, and never only as a means. If private banking provides the necessary support for public banking, then although a minority pays for the majority, the same minority gains access to the public samples, just like anyone else.

If the cord blood bank does not exploit the parent's vulnerability by using manipulative advertising and genuine informed consent is achieved, i.e., the parent making the decision to cryo-preserve his or her newborn's cord blood is aware of the unlikelihood of use (including the cases in which it cannot be used), and the alternatives in case of illness (e.g., bone marrow from a close relative), then parents choosing to bank their newborn's cord blood are making an autonomous decision, according to accepted standards of medical ethics. Although it is highly unlikely that the specific sample that they have stored will ever be used, it *is* remotely possible, and they *are* bringing themselves closer to achieving their goal of "biologic insurance" – even if it is not their own biology.

5 Summary

An argument can currently be made for the existence of cord blood banks that work as both private and public banks. I use the word "currently" as I believe that this situation is already changing and will continue to change. As evidence of the advantages of cord blood transfers increases, additional pressure will be placed on decision-makers to shift their priorities and provide greater support for public banking. In order to be considered ethical, these banks would have to promote informed consent, to the best of their ability. They would also have to refrain from manipulative (and often false) advertising. It remains to be seen whether people would continue to privately bank blood, once they both had the necessary information and the knowledge that public cord blood was available. As banking cord blood seems to be an emotional decision, I believe that some parents would continue to bank cord blood privately, as long as this option is available.

Private cord blood banks, as they currently exist, fail to comply with accepted practices of medical ethics. They use manipulative advertising techniques and do not supply patients with information necessary to achieve informed consent. They exploit the vulnerability of parents who need to make a quick decision during a stressful point in their lives. In addition, private cord banks do not promote justice – they allow only those with financial means (for whom generally a matching sample can be found more easily to begin with) to store cord blood. In cases of directed use, this puts those families who cannot afford to store their newborn's cord blood at a disadvantage compared to other families. Rei (2010) also points out that the existence of private cord blood banks (that he refers to as 'family banks') works against altruistic parents who might consider donating their newborn's cord blood to a public bank. In accordance with the universal maxim - it would be difficult to claim that organizations running private cord blood banks would accept all organizations working in the same way - providing a service that is considered by major medical organizations to be futile. Lastly, private cord blood banks treat people as an end – parents are manipulated to believe that not storing their newborn's cord blood is a mistake they could regret for the rest of their lives, should their child, G-d forbid, ever fall ill. Providing this exaggerated and sometimes false information, they convince parents to store the cord blood, accepting their money in exchange for a service that in the vast majority of cases will prove to be completely useless.

6 Bibliography

Banking Your Newborn's Cord Blood. (2010, November). Retrieved June 14, 2011, from KidsHealth.org: http://kidshealth.org/PageManager.jsp?dn=KidsHealth&lic=1&ps=107&cat_id=20661&article_set=23018

Cells For Life. (2011). Retrieved September 6, 2011, from Cells For Life: http://www.cellsforlife.com/once-in-a-lifetime.html#target

A Theory of Justice. (n.d.). Retrieved September 18, 2011, from Wikipedia: http://en.wikipedia.org/wiki/A_Theory_of_Justice

American Academy of Pediatrics Work Group on Cord , & Blood Banking. (1999). Cord blood banking for potential future transplantation: Subject review. *Pediatrics, 104*, 116-118.

Annas, G. (1999, May 13). Waste and longing -- the legal status of placental-blood banking. *The New England Journal of Medicine, 340*, 1521-1524.

Ballen, K., Barker, J. N., Stewart, S. K., Greene, M. F., & Lane, T. A. (2008). Collection and Preservaton of Cord Blood for Personal Use. *Biology of Bood and Marrow Transplantation, 14*, 356-363.

Beauchamp, T. (1992). Manipulative Advertising. *Business and Professional Ethics Journal*, 1-22.

Beauchamp, T. (2003, October). Methods and Principles in Biomedical Ethics. *Journal of Medical Ethics, 29*(5), 269-274.

Bourque, J., & Sugarman, J. (2000). Banking on the Future. *Forum for Applied Research and Public Policy, 15*(1), 65-68.

Brand, A., Rebulla, P., Engelfriet, C., Reesink, H. W., Beguin, Y., Baudoux, E., et al. (2008). Cord blood banking. *Vox Sanguinis, 95*, 335-348.

Broxmeyer, H., Srour, E. F., Hangoc, G., Cooper, S., Anderson, S. A., & Bodine, D. M. (2003). High-efficiency recovery of functional hematopoietic progenitor and stem cells from human cord blood cryopreserved for 15 years. *Publishings of the National Academy of Sciences, 100*(2), 645-650.

Burgio, G., Gluckman, E., & Locatelli, F. (2003). Ethical reappraisal of 15 years of cord-blood transplantation. *The Lancet, 361*, 250-252.

Cogdell, K. (2009). Saving the Leftovers: Models for Banking Cord Blood Stem Cells. *Issues in Law & Medicine, 25*(2), 145-165.

Cord Blood Bank. (n.d.). Retrieved September 20, 2011, from Wikipedia: http://en.wikipedia.org/wiki/Cord_blood_bank

Fernandez, C., Gordon, K., Van den Hof, M., Taweel, S., & Baylis, F. (2003, March 18). Knowledge and attitudes of pregnant women with regard to collection, testing and banking of cord blood stem cells. *Canadian Medical Association Journal, 168*(6), 695-698.

Ferreira, E., Pasternak, J., Bacal, N., de Campos Guerra, J. C., & Mitie Watanabe, F. (1999). Correspondence: Autologous cord blood transplantation. *Bone Marrow Transplantation, 24*, 1041.

Fisk, N., Roberts, I., Markwald, R., & Mironov, V. (2005). Can Routine Commercial Cord Blood Banking Be Scientifically and Ethically Justified. *PLoS Medicine, 2*(2), 87-90.

Geva, A. (2000). *Ethics and Business* . Tel Aviv: Open University of Israel.

Gluckman, E., O'Reilly, R., Wagner, R., & Rubenstein, P. (1996). Patents versus transplants (letter). *Nature, 382*, 108.

Gonzalez-Ryan, L., Van Syckle, K., Coyne, K. D., & Glove, N. (2000, Jan/Feb). Umbilical Cord Blood Banking: Procedural and Ethical Concerns for This New Birth Option. *Pediatric Nursing, 26*(1), 105-110.

Goodpaster, K. (1991). Ethical imperatives and corporate leadership. In R. E. Freeman, *Business Ethics: the state of the art, The Ruffin Series in Business Ethics* (pp. 89-110). Oxford University Press.

Grady, D. (1998, December 1). *The Hope, and Hype of Cord Blood*. Retrieved September 19, 2011, from The New York Times: http://www.nytimes.com/1998/12/01/health/the-hope-and-hype-of-cord-blood.html

Hollands, P., & McCauley, C. (2009). Private Cord Blood Banking: Current Use and Clinical Future. *Stem Cell Reviews and Reports, 5*(3), 195-203.

John Rawls. (n.d.). Retrieved September 18, 2011, from Wikipedia: http://en.wikipedia.org/wiki/John_Rawls

Justice as Fairness. (n.d.). Retrieved September 18, 2011, from Wikipedia: http://en.wikipedia.org/wiki/Justice_as_Fairness

Kahneman, D., & Tversky, A. (1979). Prospect Theory: An Analysis of Decision under Risk. *Econometrica, 47*(2), 263-292.

Rei, W. (2010). Toward a Governance Structure Beyond Informed Consent: A Critical Analysis of the Popularity of Private Cord Blood Banking in Taiwan. *East Asian Science, Technology and Society: and International Journal*, Published Online 26 May 2010.

Rubinstein, P. (2006). Why Cord Blood? *Human Immunology, 67*, 398-404.

Saginur, M., Kharaboyan, L., & Knoppers, B. (2004). Umbilical Cord Blood Stem Cells: Issues with Private and Public Banks. *Health Law Journal, 12*, 17-34.

Samuel, G., Kerridge, I. H., & O'Brien, T. A. (2008). Umbilical cord blood banking: public good or private benefit? *MJA, 188*(9), 533-535.

Schmidt, A., Platz, A., Rutt, C., & Ehninger, G. (2010). Making the Case for Private Cord Blood Banking: Mission Failed!

Comment to Hollands and McCauley. *Stem Cell Reviews and Reports, 6*, 234-2366.

Sugarman, J., Kaalund, V., & Kodish, E. (1997). Ethical issues in umbilical cord blood banking. Working Group on Ethical Issues in Umbilical Cord Blood Banking. *JAMA, 278*, 938-943.

Sullivan, M. (2008, July). Banking on cord blood stem cells. *Nature Reviews - Cancer, 8*, 554-563.

The Nuts and Bolts of Bone Marrow Transplants. (n.d.). Retrieved September 20, 2011, from Columbia Presbyterian Medical Center: http://www.cumc.columbia.edu/dept/medicine/bonemarrow/bmtinfo.html

Values in medical ethics. (n.d.). Retrieved from Wikipedia.

Veatch, R. (1972). Medical Ethics: Professional or Universal. *Harvard Theological Review, 65*, 531-559.

Veatch, R. (1991). Medicine and Money: A Study of the Role of Beneficence in Health Care Cost Containment - Book Review. *The Journal of the American Medical Association, 265*(19), 2588.

Warwick, R., & Fehily, D. (2002). Ethics of cord blood banking. *Current Obstetrics & Gynaecology, 12*, 175-177.

Why bank cord blood? (n.d.). Retrieved September 8, 2011, from Insception Cord Blood Program - Where a promise begins: http://www.insception.com/why-bank-cord-blood

Why Choose CORD:USE Cord Blood Bank. (n.d.). Retrieved September 8, 2011, from Family Cord Blood Bank: http://familycordbloodbank.corduse.com/

Wikipedia, Immanuel Kant. (n.d.). Retrieved August 21, 2011, from Wikipedia: http://en.wikipedia.org/wiki/Immanuel_Kant

Wu, G., & Gonzalez, R. (1999). Nonlinear Decision Weights in Choice under Uncertainty. *Management Science, 45*(1), 75-85.

Yaari, M., & Bar-Hillel, M. (1984). On Dividing Justly. *Social Choice and Welfare, 1*, 1-24.

www.ingramcontent.com/pod-product-compliance
Lightning Source LLC
Chambersburg PA
CBHW020714180526
45163CB00008B/3082